The Working Drummer's Chart Book

by Joe Bergamini

Music Engraving by Dan Traglia
Book Design and Layout by Joe Bergamini
Cover design by Mike Hoff
Cover Photo by Jeff Solomon

Special thanks for suggestions, proofing, and support: Rob Wallis, Steve Smith, Dave Anthony, Mike Sorrentino, Dom Famularo, Nick Bergamini, and Kim Bergamini

Other books by Joe Bergamini are available digitally at www.hudsonmusic.com and in physical format at www.joebergamini.com

Hudson Music

Table of Contents

INTRODUCTION

Welcome to ***The Working Drummer's Chart Book***. This book is intended to serve two purposes:

1. To show you my method of making song charts for drums—a lifesaving skill for any pro drummer!

2. To provide you with a useful and fun set of drum charts that demonstrates this approach, while giving you a set of charts that can be useful for practice and gigs.

This book contains a small part of the collection of shorthand drum charts I've accumulated over the years for various gigs, including club dates, corporate gigs, bar gigs, tribute band concerts, and more. There are times when I've been called to play gigs where I need to play 20 or 30 songs I've never played (or sometimes heard) before, most often with no rehearsal. This can be a daunting task, and if I had to rely on my memory, I might avoid some of these situations and turn down the work. However, with the ability to create quick, accurate charts, I'm able to take the gig with confidence: A little homework will give me the road maps I need to play the show successfully, and hopefully enjoy myself!

These charts are not transcriptions. I love transcriptions (and have written a few books of them!) but in most cases on these types of gigs, I don't want a transcription. Why? For a couple reasons:

1. I don't want my head buried in a chart. I need to use my ears to determine whether or not the band is playing the arrangement I have learned, and I need to stay locked in with the leader/MD for information. They might want a tempo adjustment, or they might change the arrangement on the fly (for instance by calling an added solo, or extending a chorus). You can't assume everything will be played like the recording you learned. Of course, this does depend on the gig. If you are on a tribute band gig at a theater, it is probable that you will know the exact arrangements of the songs you'll be playing, and have a set list. But even then, I've had changes called on the fly.

2. In most cases on corporate gigs and club dates, I don't always need to play the parts note-for-note (although I do try to write out the most important grooves and fills pretty close to the recording). A transcription can actually be problematic by taking too much of my attention away from what is happening on the bandstand. I want a road map with key information that I can glance at while keeping in musical contact with the other players.

3. These charts are really just a way to remember the basic outline of the song, along with the most important information: tempo, style, groove, and expected arrangement/form.

ELEMENTS OF THE CHARTS

Style indicator: At the top of each chart (and this goes for my charts and most pro charts) there is a simple style indicator. This is very helpful information. Sometimes this could be a specific style or groove, like "bossa nova," or it could be a style with a description of the general vibe of the song, like "mellow rock" or "hard rock."

Tempo: Metronome marking is crucial information. I find this especially important when doing a gig where I have had to learn many songs without much (or any) rehearsal time. If counting off the song, I always reference my metronome first. Even if the bandleader or MD has counted the song off (or started it), I usually "check in" with the metronome just to see where it's laying. I keep a Tama Rhythm Watch mounted just under my hi-hat (left of the snare drum), so I can easily start and stop it in time to reference tempo.

Song Sections/Rehearsal Letters/A-B-C: Having an outline of the form is probably the most important part of these charts, just like a lead sheet fills that function on a jazz gig. I usually use A for the verse, B for the chorus, and C for a bridge, but it can vary. I also use "Intro," "Guitar Solo," "Outtro," or other form indicators sometimes, rather than letters, if I feel it makes the chart clearer.

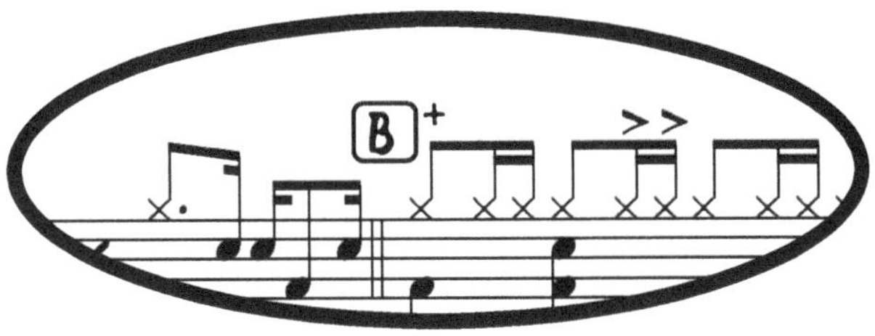

What to write out? I always write out the main grooves. If there are fills that are essential to the song—or if there are fills I just want to play note-for-note—I will write those out. Certain figures where I want to replicate what was played on the recording also get written. Beyond that, I employ shorthand to keep all charts to one page if possible.

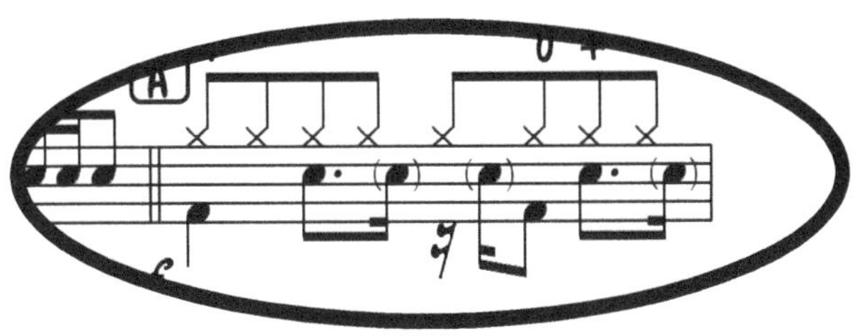

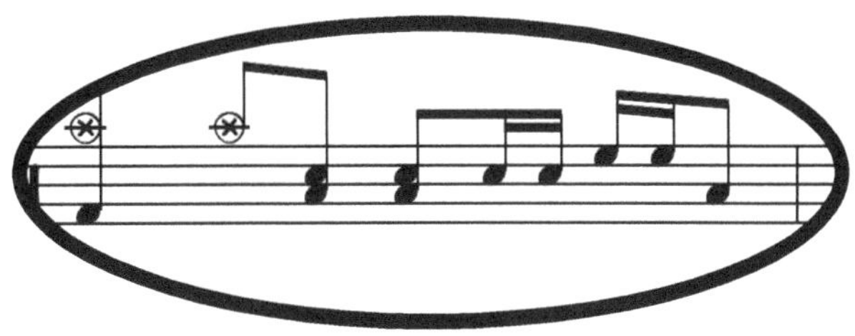

"Play 8" – "2 More" shorthand: Using "Play #" is one of the quickest ways to save space and convey basic information on my charts. But I always consider how I am breaking up these sections. I always try to make my written chart shorthand match the song phrasing. Therefore, if there is an 8-bar verse, but in one of the verses they add two bars, I'll often write "Play 8" followed by "2 More" to make things more clear.

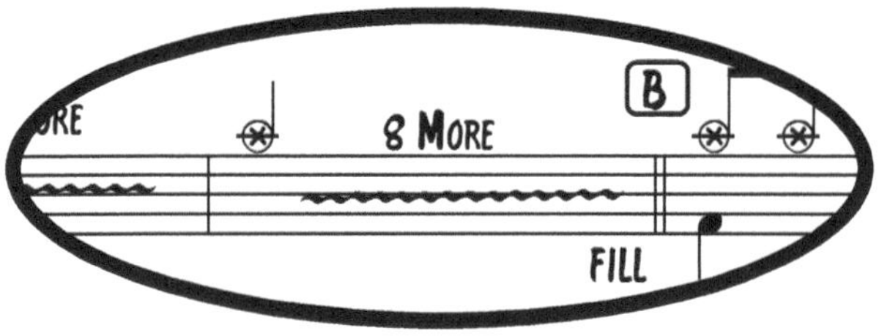

Slash notation, ensemble figures: In certain charts, I'll employ slash notation (meaning "play the appropriate groove here") rather than "Play #." This gives me flexibility to show ensemble figures quickly.

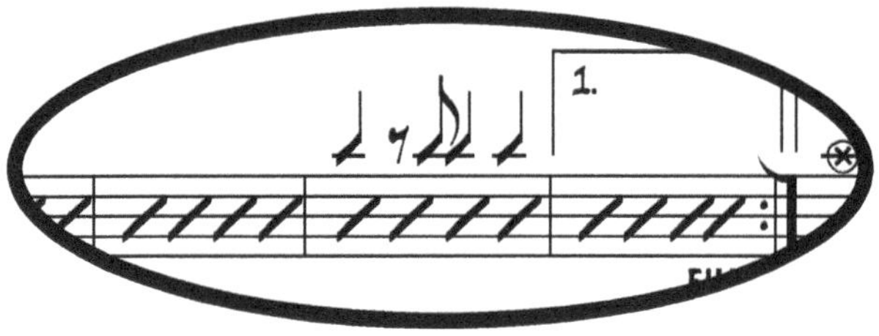

Ensemble figures come in two basic flavors (for me, anyway):

1. Big notes written on the snare drum line mean "these are figures the entire band is playing, and you must play them as well." In a jazz setting, you might also need to set them up. Often these ensemble notes are written with large slashed noteheads.

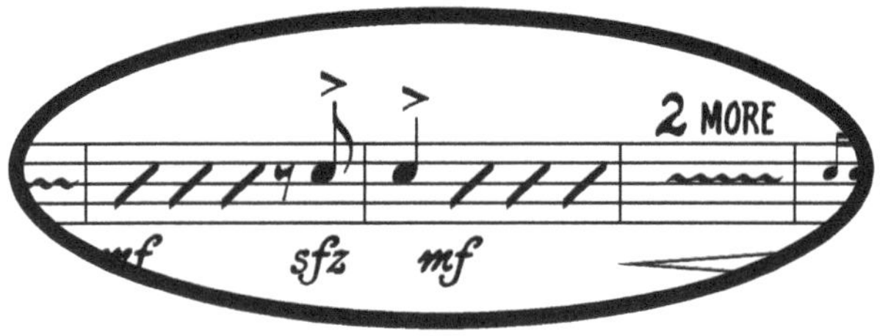

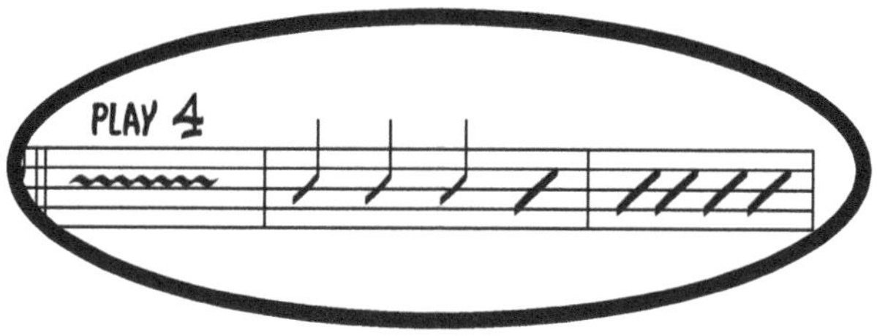

2. Small notes written above a bar of slash notation means "all or part of the band is playing these figures; you should be aware of this, and maybe you want to catch some of these rhythms."

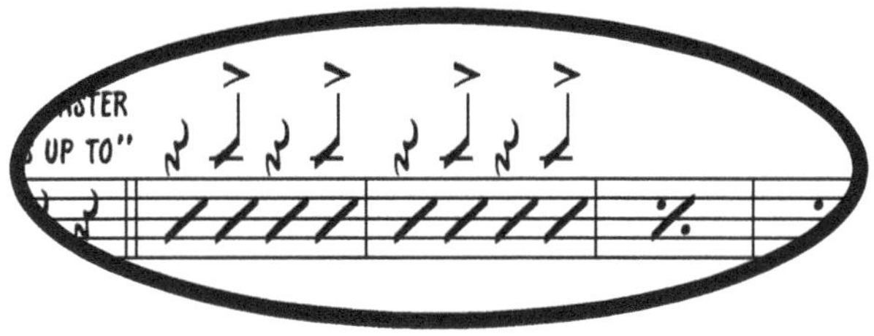

"Fill": Seems obvious, but this tells you to play a fill. It is usually written under a bar of slash notation or a "Play #." The fill is played at the end of the indicated phrase.

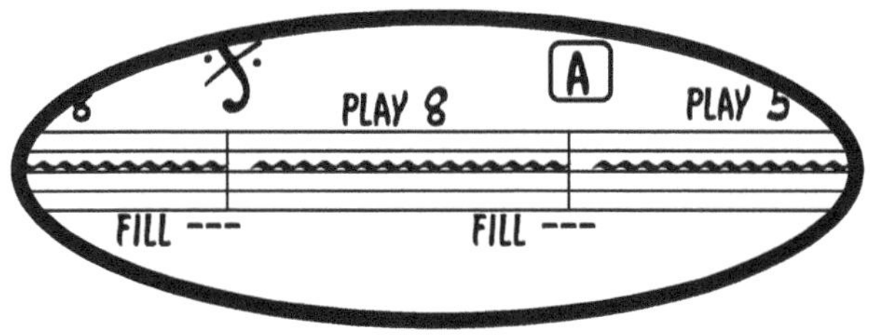

Dynamics: This important information seems to be frequently forgotten on drum charts. For some songs, such as dance or loud rock songs that don't change dynamic at all from forte, I may leave it out, but it's always best to have at least a starting dynamic.

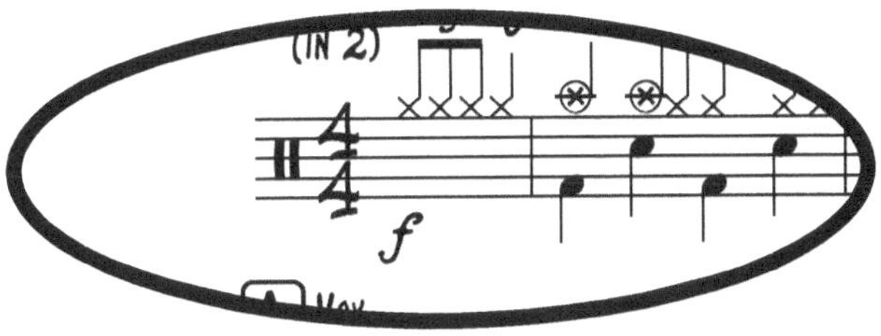

Barlines, repeats, codas, D.S., etc.: I use double barlines between the major sections of a song (A-B, verse-chorus, etc.). I also employ, and all working musicians should know, the standard devices used to shorten written charts: D.C., D.S., al Coda, and al Fine, as well as normal repeat signs and 1st/2nd endings. It is beyond the scope of this book to explain these here. If you don't know them, get with a teacher to learn or refresh your reading. And practice reading drum books with charts!

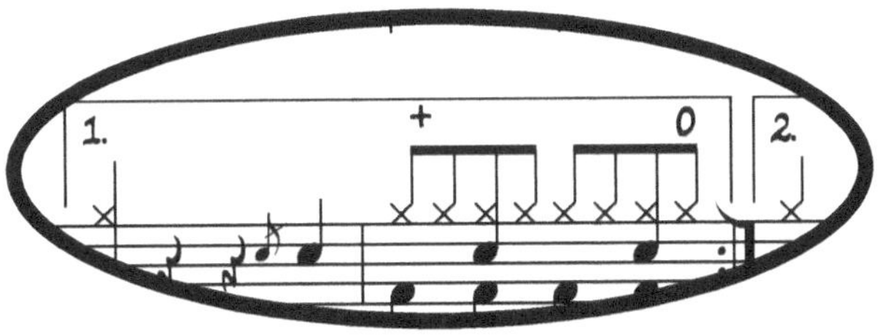

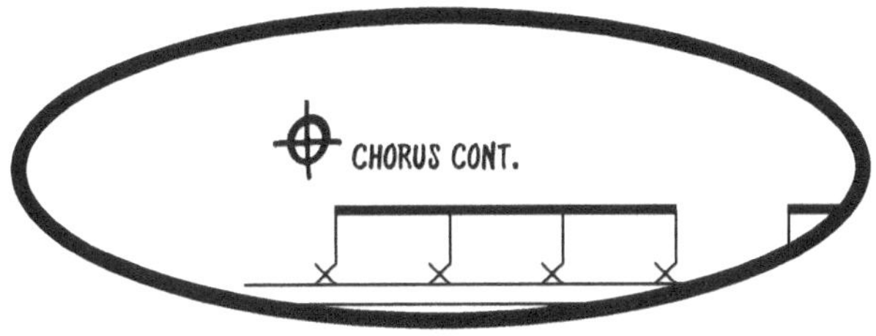

THOUGHTS ON NOTATION

All stems up? Hands up and feet down? Hi-hat/ride up and snare/kick down? Which is correct?

The answer is they are all correct. I think the focus of any drum chart, whether transcription or road map, is to be clear and easy for the user. Therefore, I base my organization, stemming, and layers on clarity. If the hi-hat is playing straight eighths with the snare and kick playing an interacting pattern underneath, I will often put the hi-hat stems up and the other stems down. For a linear David Garibaldi-type groove, I would put all stems up. For a double bass groove with steady sixteenths, I'd put the sixteenths stems down and the hands stems up—the reader can quickly glean that the feet play steady sixteenths, and he/she can focus on reading the hands. However, if notating a Simon Phillips-style fill incorporating toms and two bass drums playing figures between them, I would write all those stems up to show the full interplay and rhythm. Clarity is the focus. If busy, layered patterns are being played, don't default to all stems up. It can be confusing to read, especially on the gig.

DRUM KEY

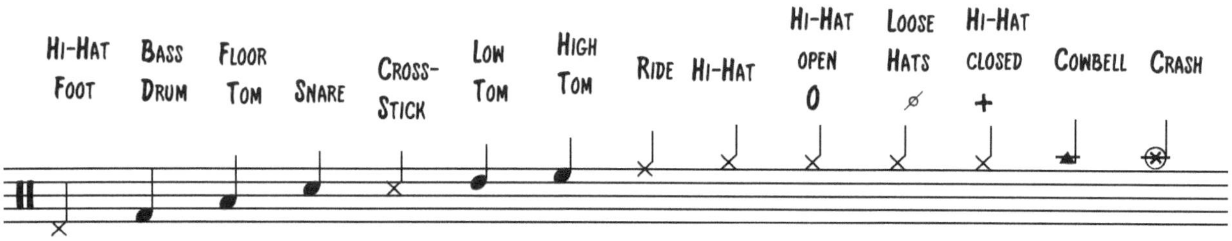

USING THE CHARTS

I like my gig charts to be clear, concise and easy to use. I've found that my iPad is the best solution for this on the gig. I used to carry around a notebook full of charts. This approach is fine if you are doing a Broadway show or a gig where the setlist won't change, and as long as you have enough light to view it (hint: bring a music stand with a light, extra batteries, and an extension cord!). But what if you're on a gig where tunes are being called? Using one of the common music organization apps such as ForScore or Paperless Music, or just using iCloud or Google Drive allows you to navigate an alphabetical list of charts and quickly tap on the one you need. I have been using the Paperless Music app, which allows you to view your entire collection of music, or make subsets and setlists as well. There are many options for this; the key is to use one that you can navigate quickly (and with one hand) so it can be used easily on stage.

As a side note, you should also be using a metronome or metronome app in conjunction with your set list (if any) and chart library. However, I wouldn't recommend trying to use the same device for both. You won't have enough time on the gig to seamlessly switch from the metronome app to the song charts. I use a Tama Rhythm Watch, which I like for several reasons. First, the button on it is big enough to start and stop during songs. The unit mounts with a special bracket right to my hi-hat stand, and it can be programmed with a set list order of tempos if needed. You can also use a phone app on a device other than the iPad/tablet you're using for your charts. Be sure to charge all your devices, or plug them in during the gig! See "The Gig Rig" section at the end of this book for more information.

HANDWRITTEN CHARTS

Here I have included a few of my handwritten charts. I still prefer to make my charts by hand, and often this is what I am looking at onstage, after it has been scanned for viewing on my tablet. To make the rest of the charts in the book clear and professional, we engraved them. Either handwritten or engraved charts work for performance, as long as they are clear and correct. If you are very fast with Finale, Sibelius, or your preferred notation software, you might like to create your charts directly in the software. Due to all the shorthand involved in making the charts that are covered in this book, I find doing them by hand faster. You can always engrave them later. The same goes for transcriptions.

Also, whether you write or engrave your charts, *save them*! Create a database of charts that you can use and trade with other players. You never know when a song will be called again. My library of charts has grown over the years into hundreds of songs, and has saved me not only many hours of repeated work, but has also saved me on the bandstand.

Following these few handwritten charts is the main section of the book with the engraved charts. I hope these are helpful and create the start of your own library of song charts!

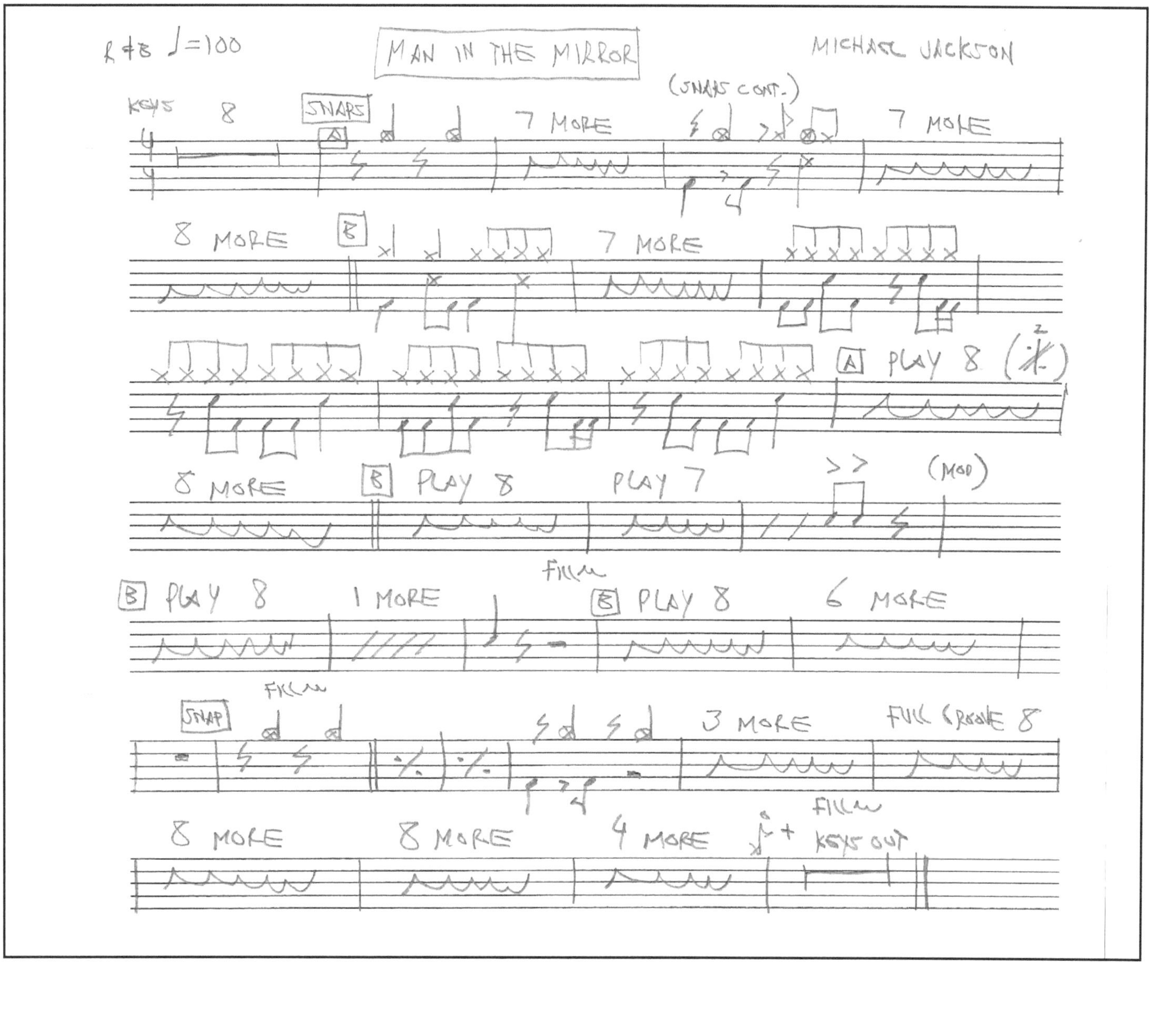

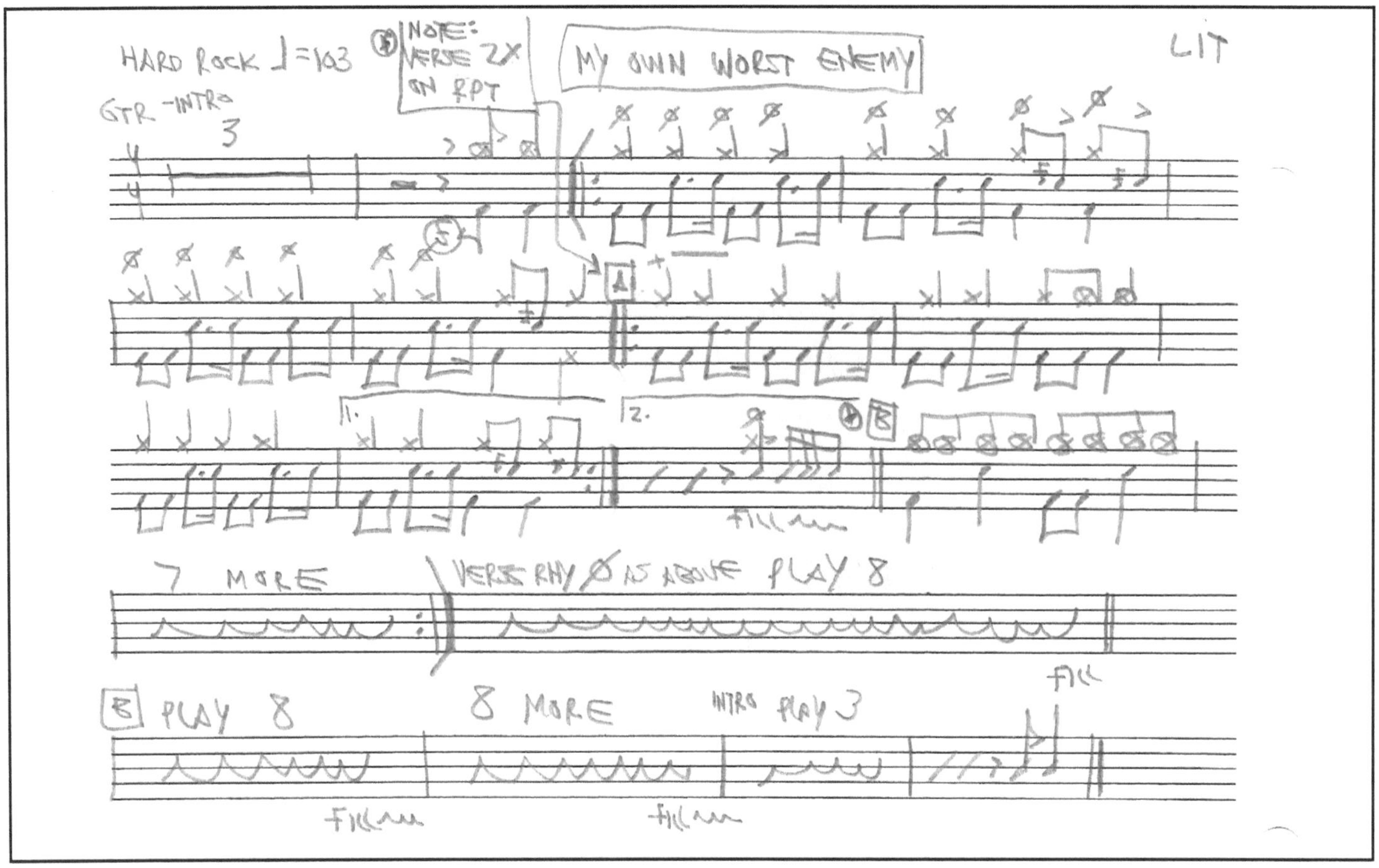
HARD ROCK ♩=103
NOTE: VERSE 2X ON RPT
MY OWN WORST ENEMY
LIT
GTR-INTRO
3
A
1.
2.
FILL
B
7 MORE
PLAY 8
B PLAY 8
8 MORE
INTRO PLAY 3
FILL

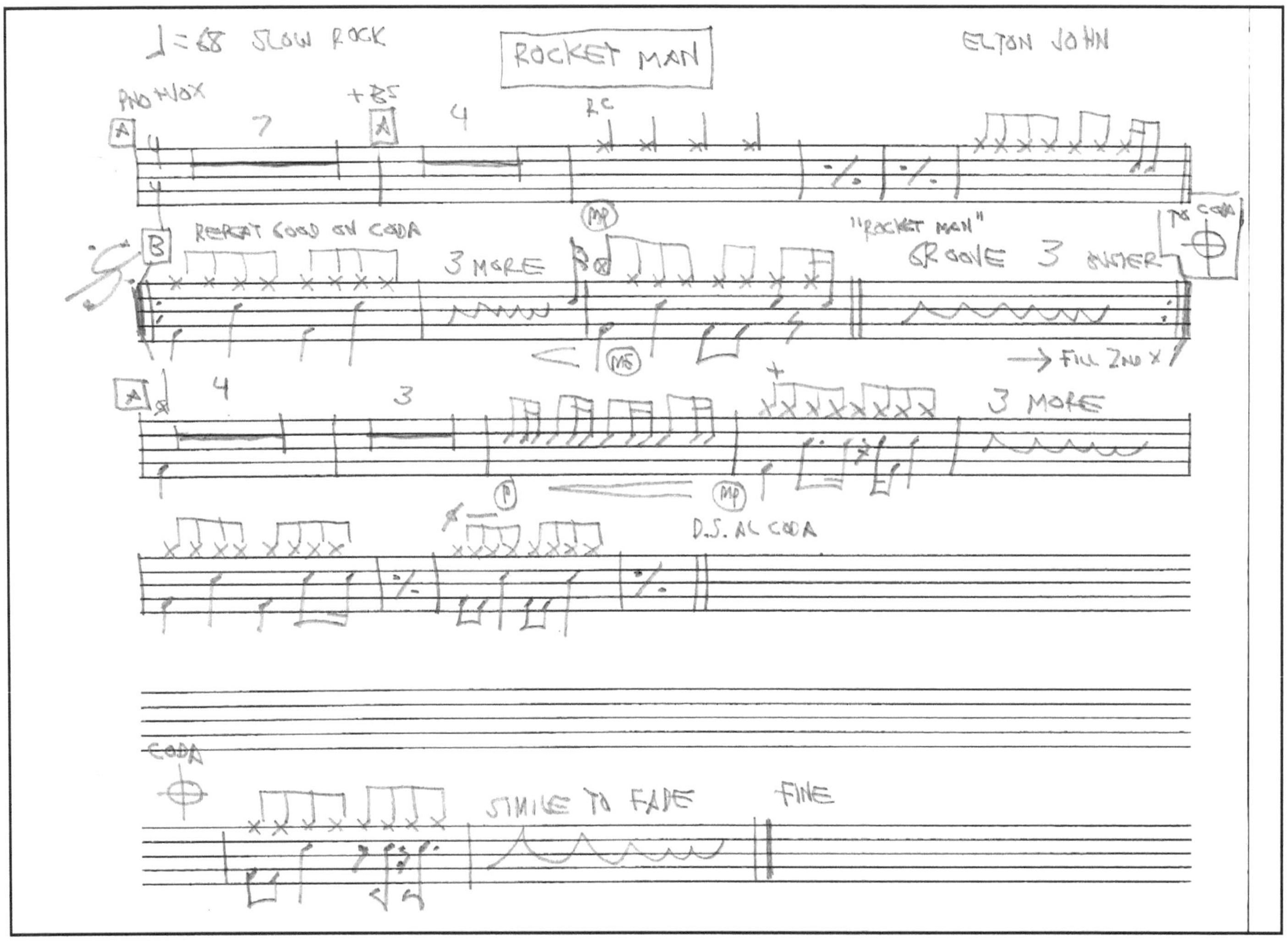
♩=68 SLOW ROCK
ROCKET MAN
ELTON JOHN
PNO+VOX
+BS
A
7
4
RC
B
3 MORE
"ROCKET MAN"
GROOVE 3
TO CODA
FILL 2ND X
4
3
3 MORE
D.S. AL CODA
CODA
SIMILE TO FADE
FINE

THE CHARTS

The following pages contain 26 drum charts that I made for gigs of different kinds, with the one common denominator being I knew I would not have a rehearsal. These charts, and hundreds of others like them in my library, are a huge asset in feeling confident on the bandstand. I chose songs that represent different styles that come up on club dates and corporate gigs (hard rock, country, hip-hop, pop, classic R&B, disco, swing), while trying to choose songs that are called fairly often.

Are You Gonna Go My Way

Driving Rock

Lenny Kravitz

Rock

♪ = 142

Bohemian Rhapsody

Queen

BUILD ME UP BUTTERCUP

R&B SHUFFLE

THE FOUNDATIONS

CAN'T STOP THE FEELING

DANCE/POP

♩= 117

J. TIMBERLAKE

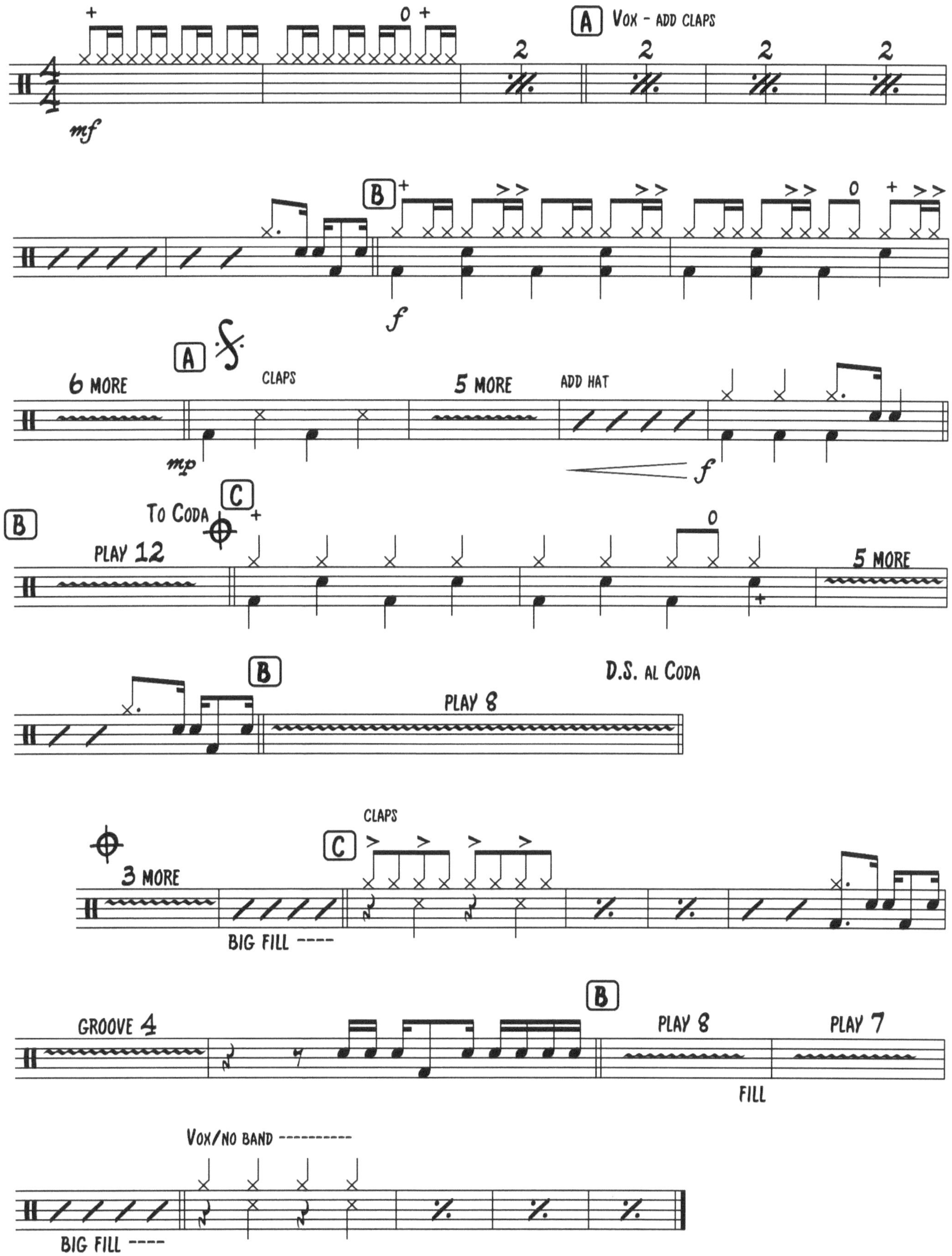

Country Two-Step

♩= 170

Chicken Fried

Zac Brown

Rock

♩= 92

Closing Time

(single edit)

Semisonic

Rock

Dreams

Fleetwood Mac

♩ = 120

Hip-Hop
♩= 88

Empire State of Mind

Jay Z/Alicia Keys

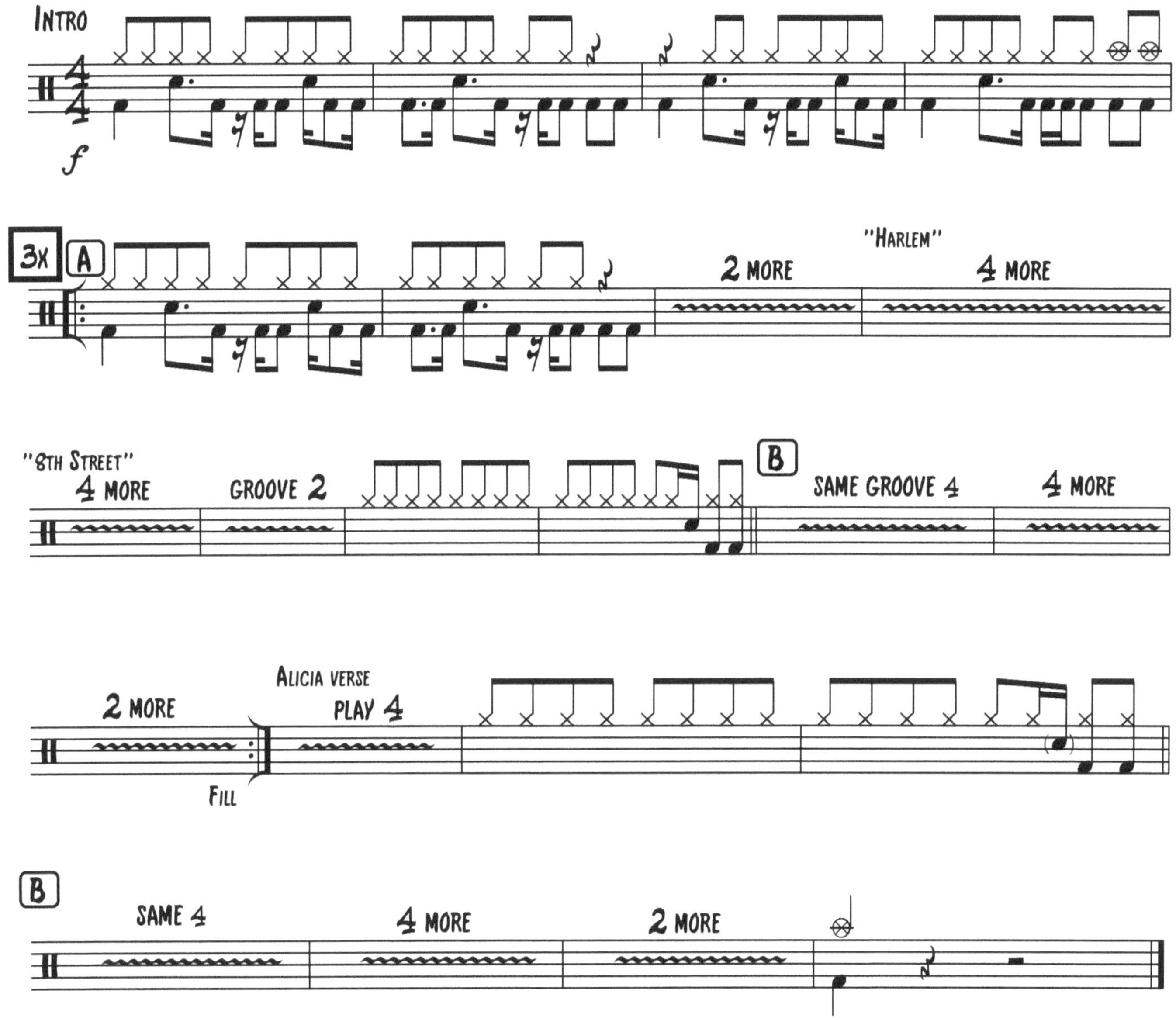

HEAVY ROCK SHUFFLE (NO HI-HAT)

♩ = 140

EX'S & OH'S

ELLE KING

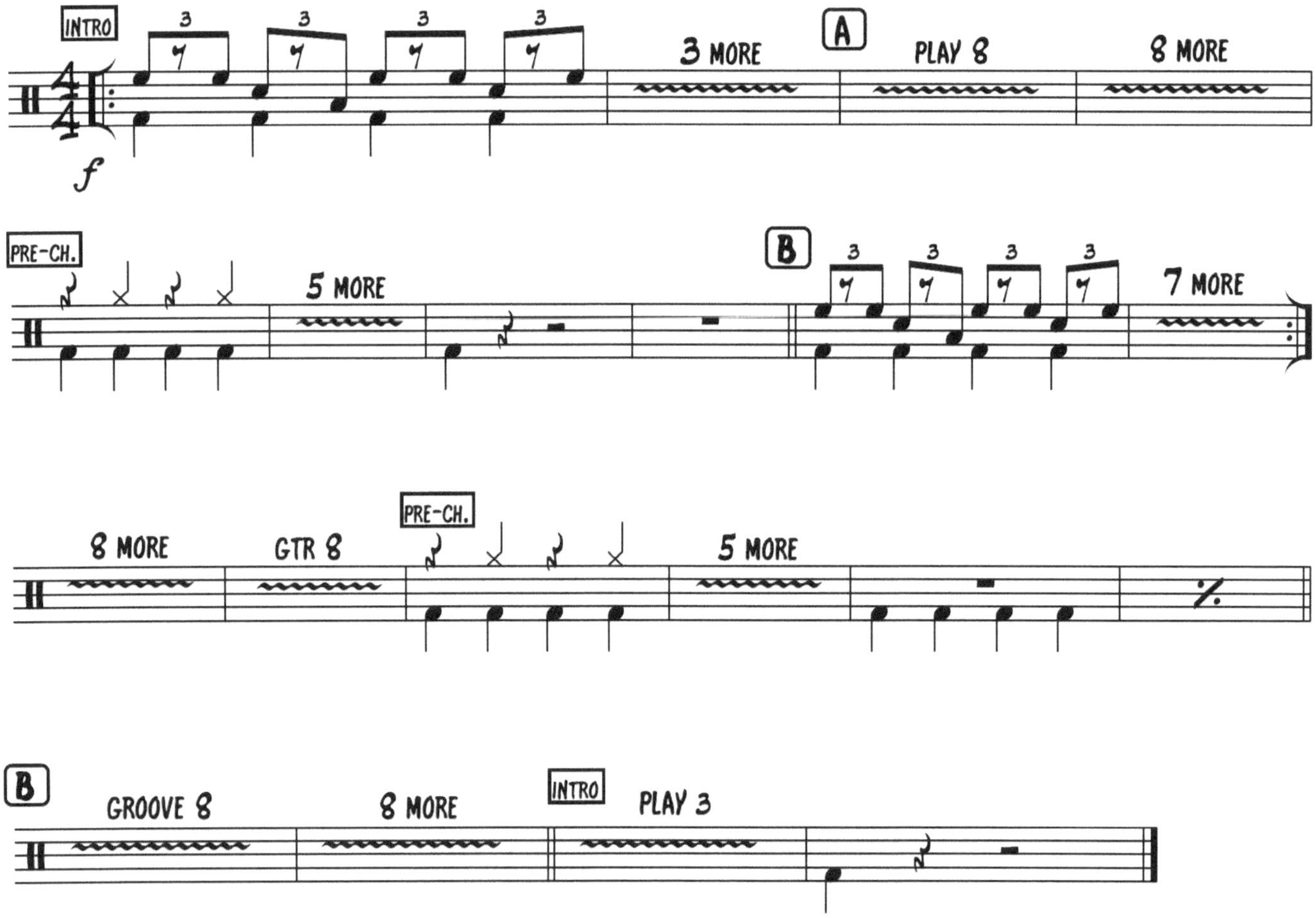

POP/DANCE

FIREWORK

KATY PERRY

♩= 124

FRIENDS IN LOW PLACES

COUNTRY

♩ = 110

GARTH BROOKS

Fast Rock Shuffle

I Know A Little

Lynryd Skynyrd

Hard Rock

Jessie's Girl

Rick Springfield

♩ = 132

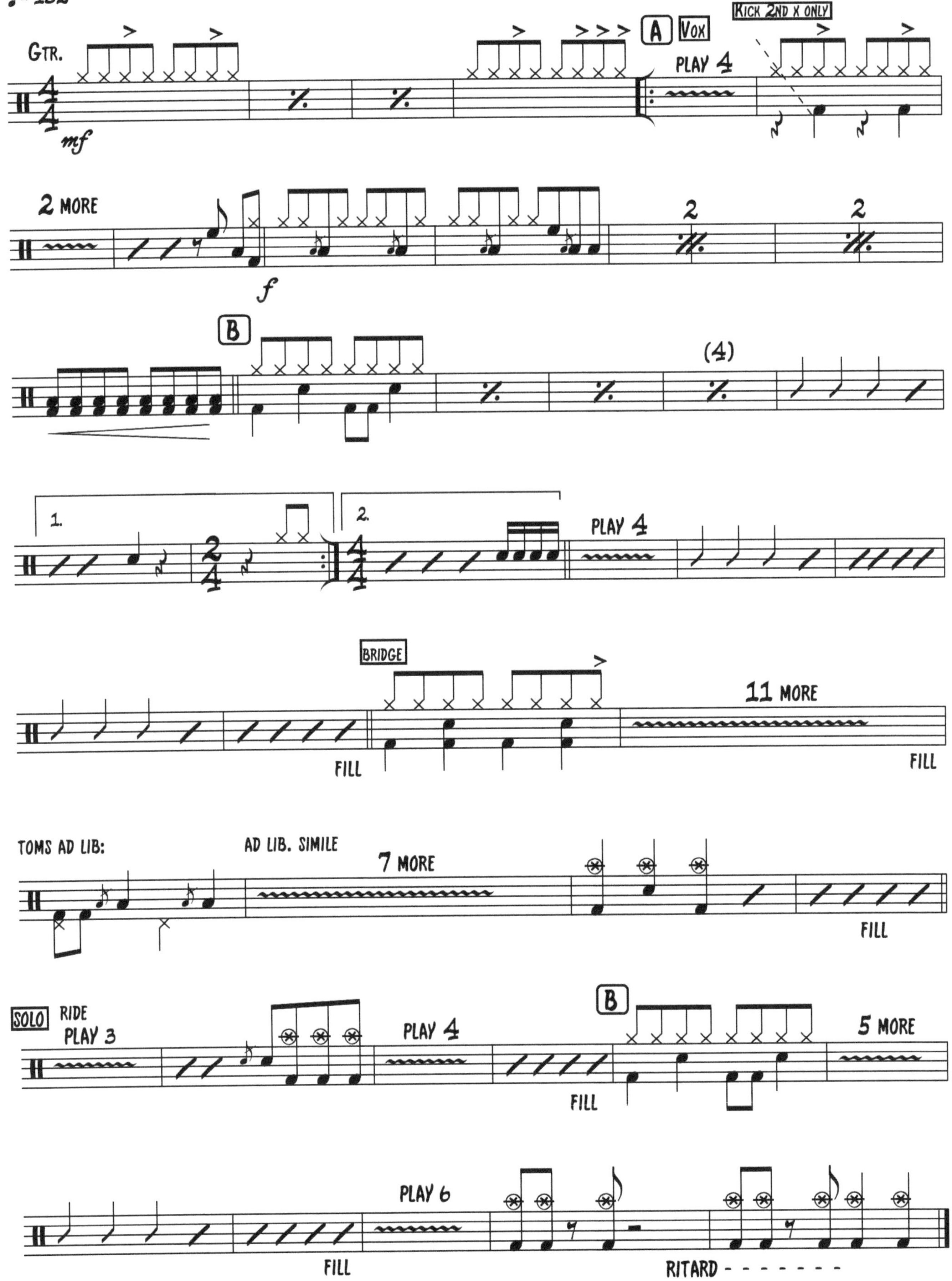

R&B

♩= 114

LADY MARMALADE

PATTI LABELLE

Disco

♩ = 126

Last Dance

Donna Summer

ROCK/DANCE

♩ = 114

LET'S DANCE

(SINGLE VERSION)

DAVID BOWIE

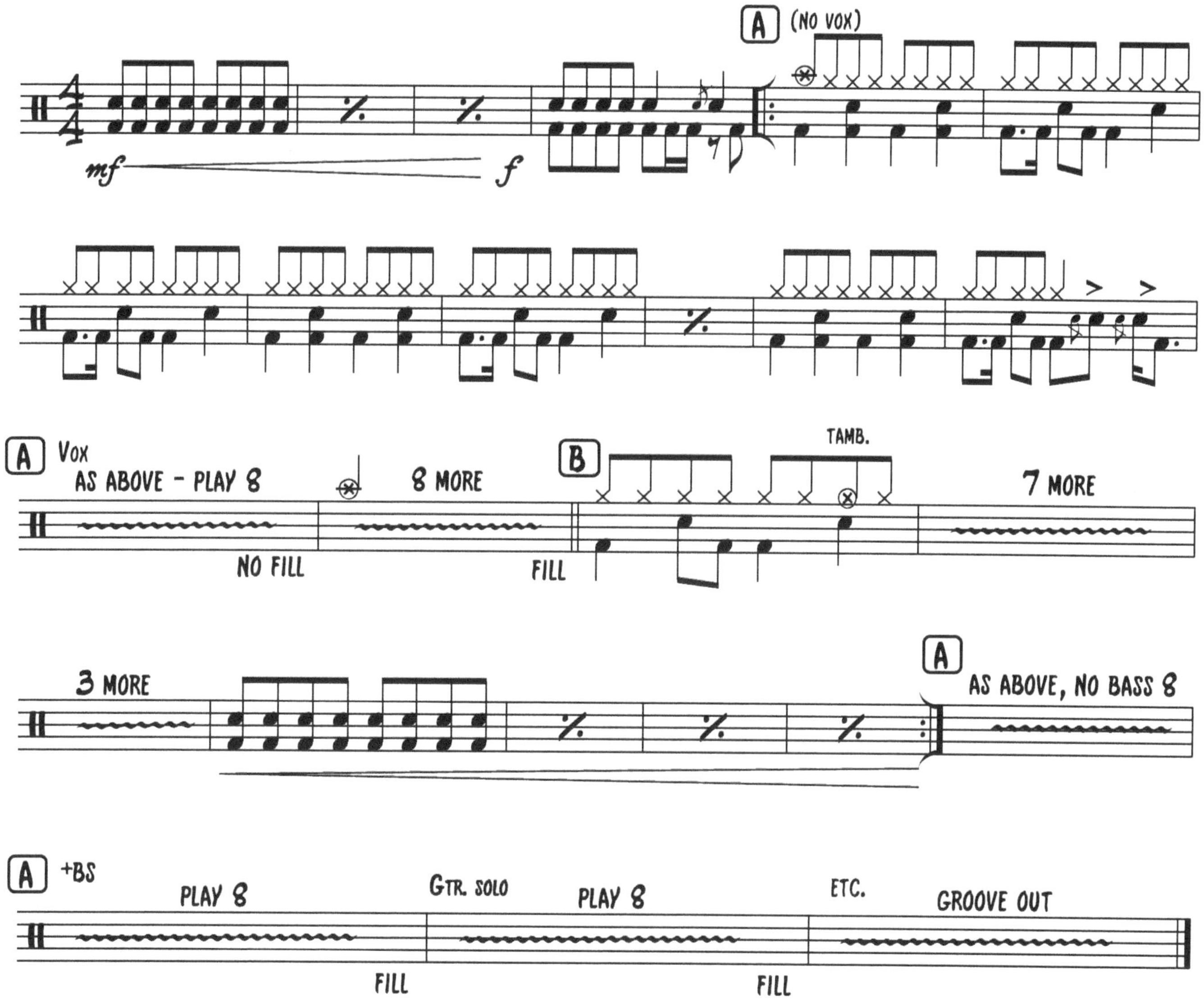

Like a Virgin

Pop

♩ = 120

Madonna

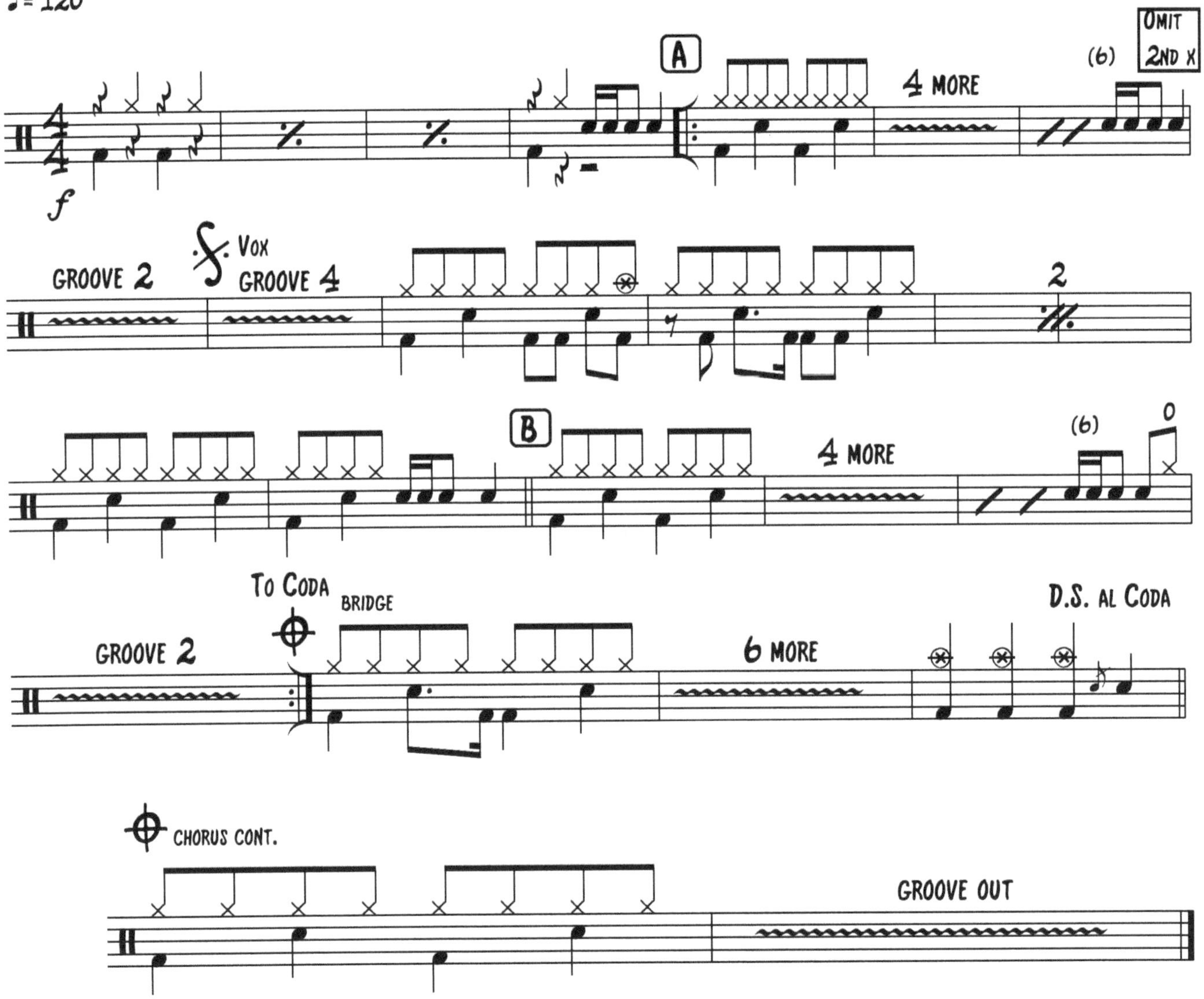

Love Shack

Rock
♩ = 132

The B-52's

Pop/Dance

♩= 128

Moves Like Jagger

Maroon 5

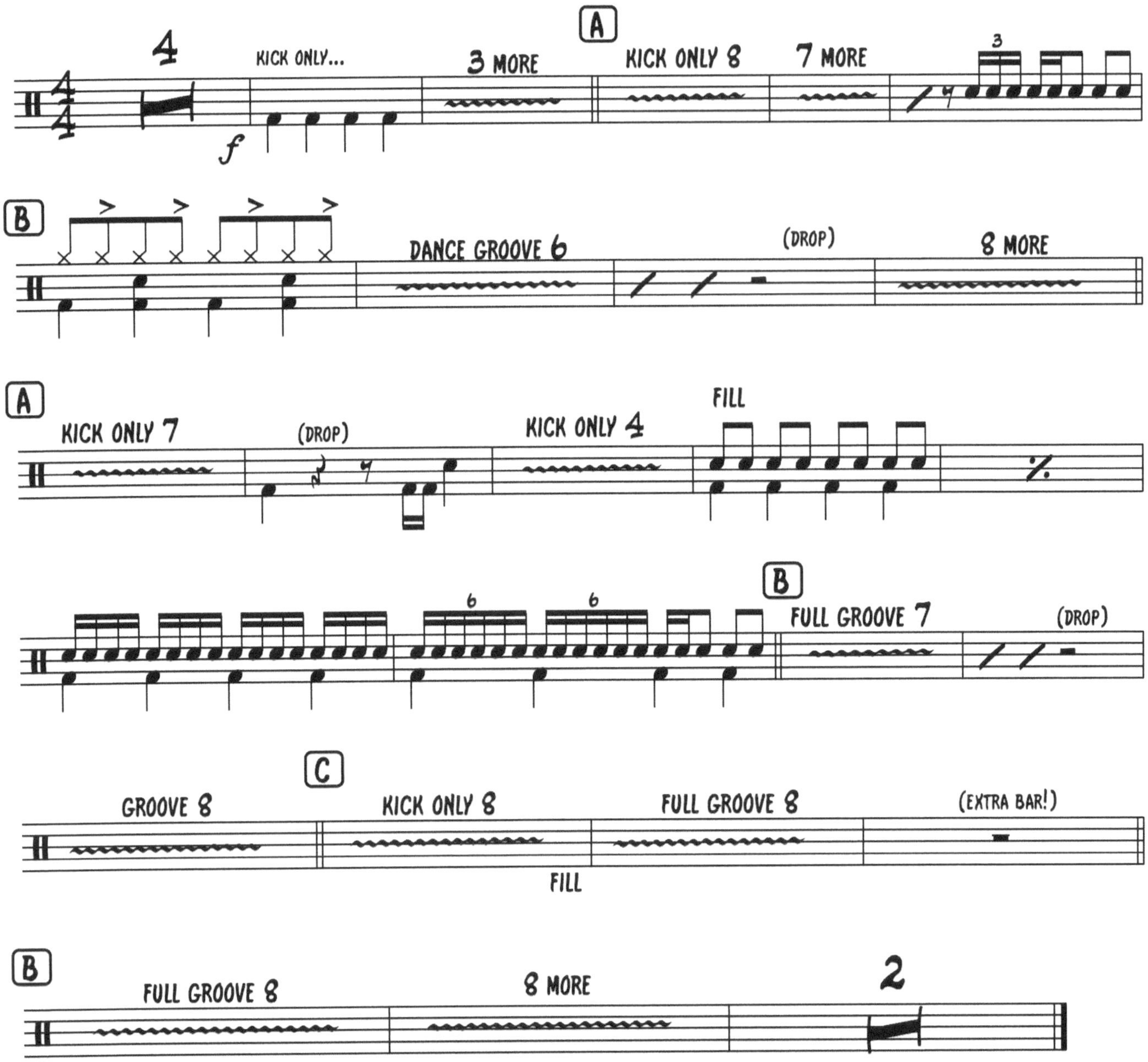

New York, New York

Frank Sinatra

Swing ♩= 108

Raise Your Glass

Rock/Pop
♩= 122

Pink

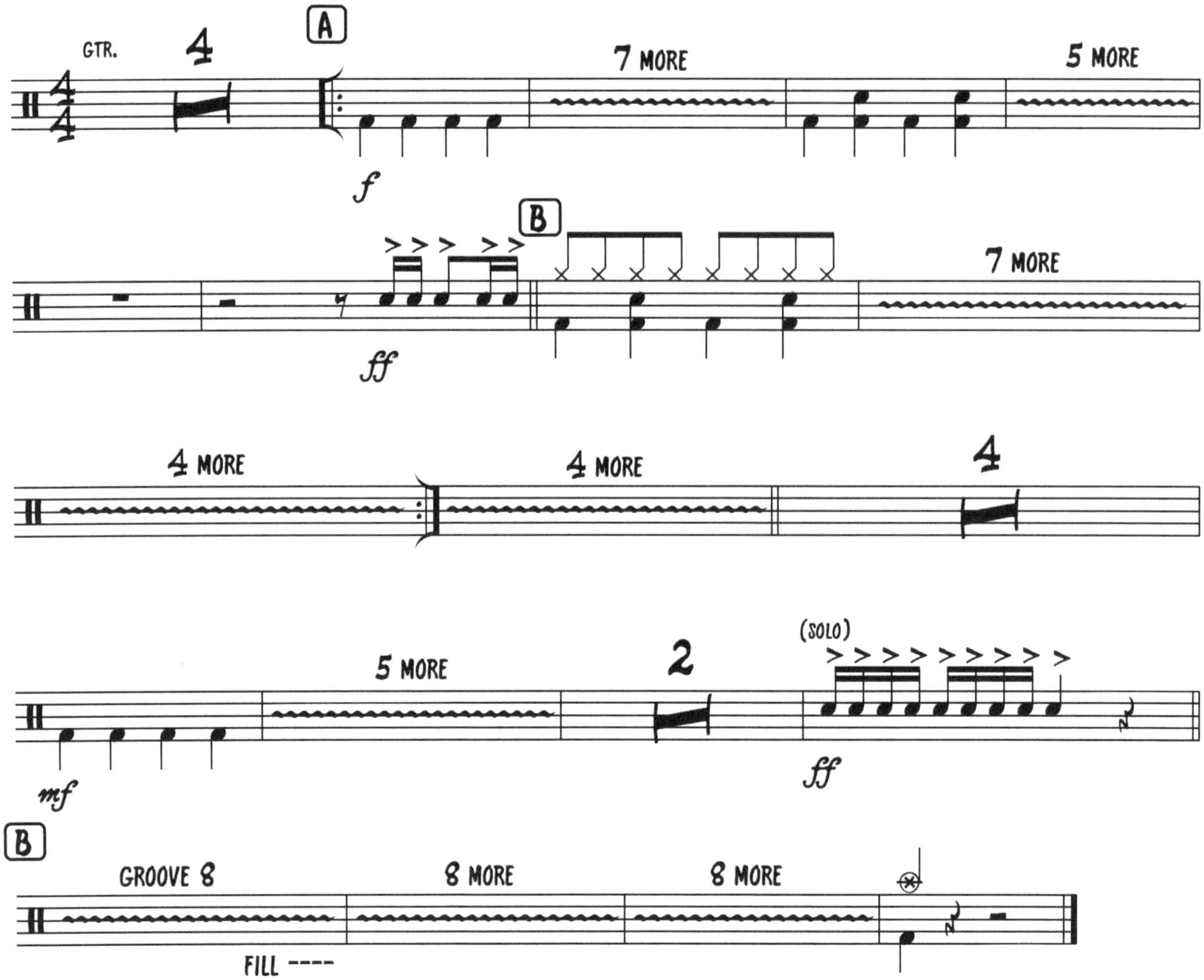

ROLLING IN THE DEEP

POP/DANCE
♩= 105

ADELE

Pop

♩ = 160

Shake it Off

Taylor Swift

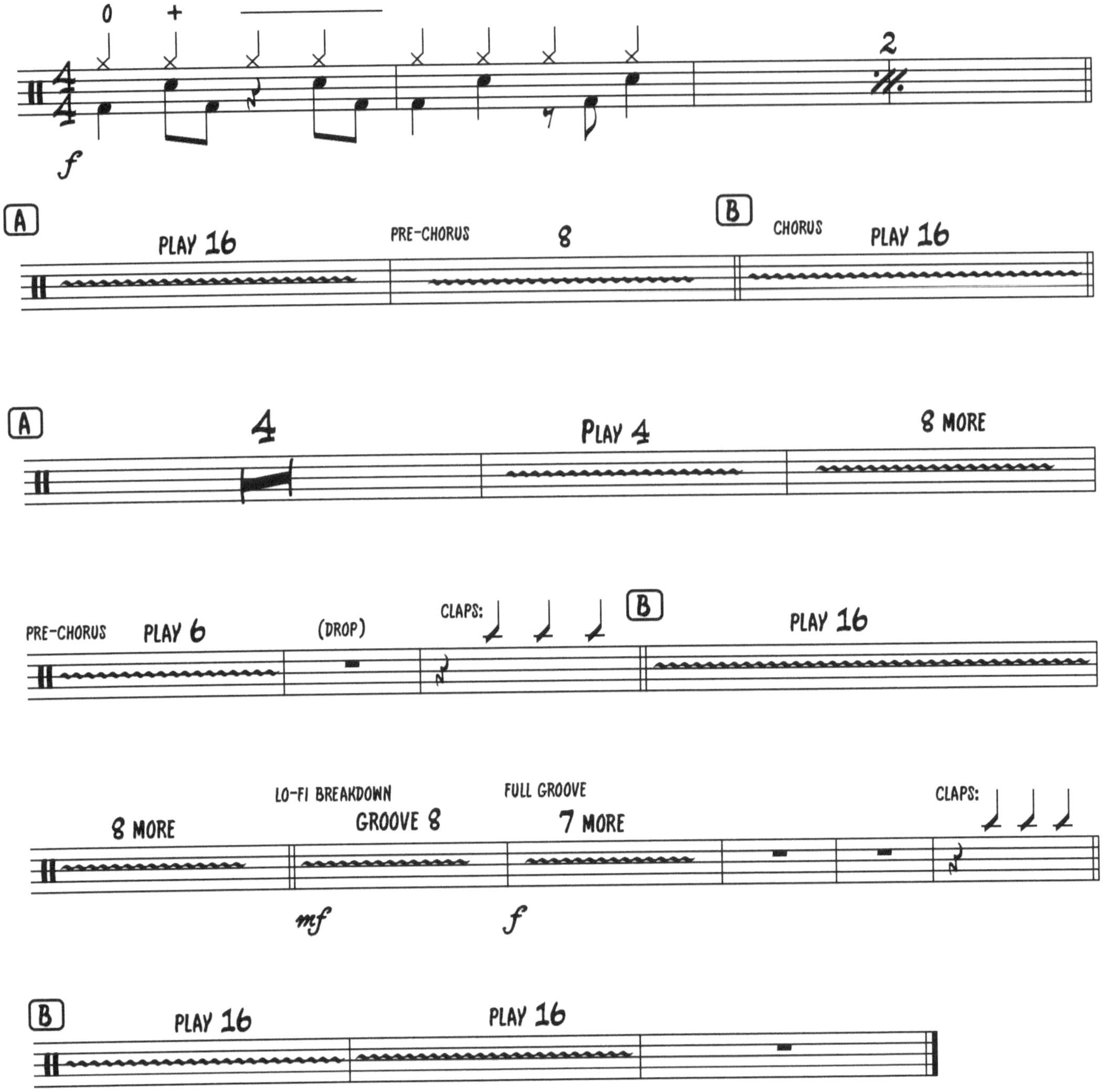

Rock

♩ = 130

Shut Up and Dance

Walk the Moon

Sir Duke

Stevie Wonder

Swing Funk

♩= 107

SWING ♪s - AD LIB HAT

Funky dance groove
♩ = 115

Uptown Funk

Mark Ronson/Bruno Mars

THE GIG RIG

This section deals with your setup as it applies to using charts. If you are playing the type of gigs where charts can be used, or are required, it is essential that you have an effective setup for using them. There are also a few items that are indispensable for reference and emergency use on any gig, so let's take a look.

Metronome

A physical metronome is a must-have item for every drummer. When it comes to metronomes in the pro world, the Tama Rhythm Watch (RW200) reigns supreme. Nearly every Broadway conductor uses it on the podium to reference tempo, and some use it for an audible click that enters the monitor system for the orchestra. Countless touring drummers use it for reference in starting and playing songs at an exact tempo every night. There are other metronomes that are similar, but the Rhythm Watch is the one I see everywhere. This is because it is just the right size to be convenient but not too small to see and use on the gig, it has the right features to program a set list, is backlit for dark places, has a rugged button that can be hit during performance easily, and (last but not least) there is an available mounting package that lets you put it right where you need it on the drumset, and utilize it during performance. Mine is mounted right under my hi-hat. I use it to start songs, check tempo mid-song, and reference tempo between songs

As mentioned, there are other good metronomes, but the features of the Rhythm Watch are what make it so popular in work environments. Tama also makes a smaller version (Tama Mini Rhythm Watch, RW30) which is good for reference and desk use, and it can fit in your pocket. If you are playing gigs where you aren't playing to a click and it is up to you to set the tempo, you may feel you don't need a metronome for reference. That is every drummer's call, of course, but in the pro world of hired guns, the stakes are high, and you must come in at the right tempo every time. I've personally asked Steve Gadd (with Eric Clapton and James Taylor), Simon Phillips (with Toto), and Keith Carlock (with Steely Dan) if they use a metronome to reference tempo before counting off songs on tour, and all said yes. Chuck Burgi (Billy Joel) played the entire *Movin' Out* show on Broadway to the Rhythm Watch (except for the songs that had a click track) because the dancers onstage needed the songs to be at exactly the same tempo every night. Pro drummers play songs at the right tempo. Nothing sounds more amateurish than a band playing songs too fast in performance. So keep this in mind, even if you are playing small venues with a local band. No gig is too unimportant to sound like a pro!

Metronome Apps

There are countless metronome apps available for all types of devices including phones, tablets, and computers. Having a metronome on your phone is a great idea for every drummer. While I still prefer the reliability of the physical, kit-mounted Rhythm Watch, the phone app comes in very handy. At the time of this writing, some of the popular ones are Tempo, Polynome, SYNKD, Metro Time, and Google Metronome, but there are dozens of others. Tempo has some nice features where you can add set lists and scroll through them in order. If you prefer the app-based metronome solution, you can use it for the same purposes as described for the physical metronome, above.

Chart Storage and Use Apps

On the gig, you need a clean and reliable way to switch between charts. If you have a pre-determined set list, it is fairly easy to put your charts in order before the show, but if you are on a gig where the tunes are being called, you need an index that is easy to scroll through to find a chart quickly. I am aware of the apps

ForScore and Paperless Music, both of which accomplish these tasks nicely, allowing you to save set lists and also access your entire library of charts, and group it into categories.

Other Apps
When making charts, probably the biggest time saver for me is a looping function in a music app, as well as the ability to slow a track down. The Amazing Slow Downer is my choice for this, but there are others.

Physical Charts
If you are using physical/paper charts, prepare them in such a way that you will be organized on the gig. For me, this means never using a pile of loose papers if I can avoid it. I use either a folder with the charts placed in order, or a book/notebook. Sometimes I will have some loose papers on my stand even though I am using an iPad for my charts. These sheets could be additional information such as a possible song list, set list, details about the gig, last-minute charts provided by the MD, etc. I keep a couple of notebook clips in my cymbal bag to organize these papers in order if using them alongside my iPad. A folder is sometimes provided by the musical director on certain gigs, and usually—if the MD has prepared properly—the multi-page charts will fold out on your stand to eliminate page turns.) If I am providing my own charts, I place them in sheet protectors in a binder. This keeps everything in order, stops it from blowing away in the wind, and makes for easy page turns while playing.

Music Stand with Stand Light
This may seem obvious, but you should invest in a good, collapsible music stand with a stand light. I prefer the newer LED stand lights, but you must always carry spare batteries for them, or an AC adaptor if possible. For years I used a regular Broadway-style incandescent stand light, but carrying around the spare bulbs was a drag.

Device to View Charts: Laptop, iPad
Invest in the best and largest device you can afford for using digital charts on the bandstand. Tablets are perfect for this application, especially if you already have to use a laptop for other electronic tasks on the gig. Tablets can be mounted with specially-made hardware and mounts from practically anywhere on your kit. You can also simply place your iPad on a music stand. Do not attempt to use a cell phone to view charts.

Other Supplies
When I am using charts on the gig, I add a few items to my "mobile gig emergency supply pack." Batteries for all devices are essential, even though I have an AC adapter for my stand lights. An extension cord or two is recommended, along with a power strip. Always have a couple pencils in your stick bag as well. Finally, Steve Smith reminded me that clothespins are also a good idea for outdoor gigs, so your music doesn't blow away if you're using paper charts!

I hope you have enjoyed the book, and that you'll find it useful in playing more gigs with confidence in your ability to make and use drum charts! Visit me at www.joebergamini.com or on social media to let me know how you're doing!

ABOUT THE AUTHOR

Joe Bergamini maintains a diverse career as a drumming performer and educator. Enjoying various styles of playing, he is most well-known for his progressive rock drumming in the bands Happy the Man and 4Front, and is the current international touring drummer for The Doo-Wop Project. Based in the New York area, Joe has worked extensively on Broadway. In 2018, he held the drum chair for the Broadway production of *Gettin' the Band Back Together*, and has also performed over 15 other shows including *Beautiful (The Carole King Musical); Hamilton; Movin' Out; Jersey Boys; Rock of Ages; In the Heights, The Lion King,* and others. He has also appeared on the first national tours of *Movin' Out, Jersey Boys* and *Beautiful,* and with the Philly Pops and the Detroit, Jacksonville, Seattle, San Diego, Indianapolis and Vancouver Symphony Orchestras.

Recognized internationally as an educator, Joe has given hundreds of drum clinics in schools, retail stores, and conventions. He has appeared at the Percussive Arts Society International Convention (PASIC), the Ultimate Drummers Weekend (Melbourne, Australia), the Cape Breton Drum Festival (Nova Scotia, Canada), KOSA (Vermont, USA), and the Sonny Emory Drum Camp (Atlanta, USA), and has done two clinic tours for Tama Drums. He has been teaching privately at his own studio for over 30 years. Among Joe's many private students who have gone on to pro careers is world-renowned jazz drummer Mark Guiliana.

Since 2015, Joe has been Education Consultant for Sabian, designing and directing the Sabian Education Network for drum teachers. As the Senior Drum Editor for Hudson Music since 2009, Joe has worked in the acquisitions, project management and editing of educational drum products from many of the world's greatest drummers, including Neil Peart, Steve Smith, Mark Guiliana, David Garibaldi, and many others. As an author, Joe has won four *Modern Drummer* Readers Poll awards for his drum books, including best drum book of 2013 for *Neil Peart: Taking Center Stage*. He is also the author or co-author of nine other books, has edited dozens more, and is co-owner (with Dom Famularo) of Wizdom Media, an independent music publisher distributed worldwide by Alfred Publishing. Joe proudly endorses Tama drums, Sabian cymbals, Vic Firth sticks, Evans drumheads, and Latin Percussion.

www.joebergamini.com
www.facebook.com/joebergaminidrums
www.instagram.com/joebergamini/
www.youtube.com/user/joebergaminidotcom

Joe would like to thank **Dan Traglia** for his assistance on this book, including doing the music engraving and proofing. Please visit him at **www.dantraglia.com** to learn more about his drumming, teaching, and more.